BERKLEE SOLO
UKULELE

Karen Hogg

To access audio visit:
www.halleonard.com/mylibrary

Enter Code
8478-8464-5108-4157

BERKLEE PRESS

Editor in Chief: Jonathan Feist
Senior Vice President of Online Learning and Continuing Education/CEO of Berklee Online: Debbie Cavalier
Vice President of Enrollment Marketing and Management: Mike King
Vice President of Academic Strategy: Carin Nuernberg
Editorial Assistant: Brittany McCorriston
Photographer: Tracy Walton
Recording Engineer: Tracy Walton, On Deck Sound Studios

ISBN 978-1-7051-4202-8

1140 Boylston Street
Boston, MA 02215-3693 USA
(617) 747-2146

Visit Berklee Press Online at
www.berkleepress.com

Study music online at
online.berklee.edu

HAL•LEONARD®
7777 W. BLUEMOUND RD. P.O. BOX 13819
MILWAUKEE, WISCONSIN 53213

Visit Hal Leonard Online
www.halleonard.com

Berklee Press, a publishing activity of Berklee College of Music, is a not-for-profit educational publisher.
Available proceeds from the sales of our products are contributed to the scholarship funds of the college.

CONTENTS

ACKNOWLEDGMENTS

Thank you to Vickie Hogg, Victor Hogg, Coleen O'Mara, Jonathan Feist, Kim Perlak, the Berklee Guitar Department, David Wallace, the Berklee String Department, Danielle Parillo, April Capone, Amanda Monaco, David Weintraub, Denise Barbarita, Dan Canon, Noah Baerman, Kate Ten Eyck, Annabel Chiarelli, Matthew LeFebvre, Middlesex Music Academy, National Guitar Workshop, and Charissa Hoffman.

This book is dedicated to my ukulele students. Because of your love for the ukulele, I have been inspired to create the content within these pages. Without your enthusiasm and commitment to the instrument, this book would not exist. Thank you.

I would also like to dedicate this book to the memory of my father, Howard Hogg. Your love, guidance, and support has made me the educator, musician, and human being that I am today. Your spirit imbues everything that I do, including this book.

INTRODUCTION

Today, the popularity of the ukulele is at an all-time high, with more people playing than ever before. The ukulele is everywhere, in schools and community centers across the United States and all over the world. Virtuoso players like Jake Shimabukuro and James Hill have added to the popularity of this sweet-sounding instrument. These musicians have also inspired budding ukuleleists to delve deeper with the instrument.

When a player gets to a point where they want to move beyond strumming basic open chords, some questions naturally arise. How do you play chords in different places on the neck? How do you create your own chord-melody arrangements? How do you execute some of the techniques that advanced players do so effortlessly? How do you apply music theory to the ukulele? In short, how do you become a musician on the ukulele?

While there are some great ukulele ensembles out there, such as the Ukulele Orchestra of Great Britain, this book will focus on ideas and techniques for solo ukulele players. The book starts with some rudimentary material to ensure the reader has an understanding of some foundational ideas. It then delves into concepts to give readers a solid foundation to begin creating, or refining, their own solo ukulele arrangements. Each concept is accompanied by musical examples to illustrate the practical application of these ideas.

HOW TO USE THIS BOOK

While this book can be gone through sequentially, from start to finish, it is also set up so that you can focus on a particular chapter or topic that you are working on at the moment. For instance, if you are working on developing various fingerstyle patterns, you can go straight to chapter 5 ("Fingerstyle Patterns"). However, it is strongly suggested that if you are unfamiliar with chord construction, begin with the first three chapters (Part I. "Chords and How They're Built"). The material in part I is foundational information that you will build upon later in the book.

There are several different sizes of ukuleles. From smallest to largest, they are: soprano, concert, tenor, baritone, and bass ukulele. The tuning for soprano, concert, and tenor ukulele is GCEA. The baritone ukulele is tuned DGBE. The tuning for the bass ukulele (a relatively new instrument, and slightly larger than the baritone) is EADG. This book is for GCEA tuning. My personal preference is for tenor ukuleles, because they offer a greater scale length and hence, more range. Some of the arrangements in this book require that you have more than twelve frets on your uke, and thus only playable on tenor or some concert instruments. Most are playable on any ukulele.

ABOUT THE RECORDINGS

To access the accompanying audio, go to www.halleonard.com/mylibrary and enter the code found on the first page of this book. This will grant you instant access to every example. Examples with accompanying audio are marked with an audio icon.

PLAYING POSITION/POSTURE

Playing an instrument has a component of physical activity. If you spend hours in a position that does not work well for your body, this can result in injury or limitations on your technique. Good posture is important.

The good news is that the ukulele, with its small body and light weight, can be played by anyone, from young children on up to nonagenarians. However, because of its small size, the uke can also be tricky to hold. Below are some suggestions for holding your ukulele. These are guidelines. I urge you to listen to your body and work with a teacher to develop good habits

While there is room for variation in how you hold the ukulele, there are some things to watch out for. Don't slouch! This can create back and neck tension. Be careful not to bend the wrist of your fretting hand too much. Also, watch that you don't press too hard into the back of the neck with your thumb. In general, watch for signs of tension. Don't ignore them, and work to alleviate tension when you are playing.

(a) Good Wrist Position

(b) Bad Wrist Position

(c) Thumb Position

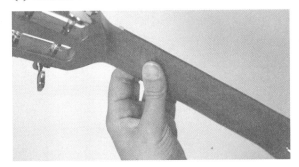

FIG. I.1. Wrist and Thumb Position

Stand up tall and hold the body of the ukulele close to you, securing it with your strumming-hand forearm.

FIG. I.2. Standing

Hold the neck of your uke gently with your fretting hand, placing your thumb in the middle of the back of the neck. Imagine you are eating a sandwich with your fretting hand. Make sure the thumb is in line with the first finger (or else the bread of your sandwich will fall apart!).

FIG. I.3. Fretting Hand Position

Sit up straight, and rest the lower bout of your ukulele on your right thigh. Make sure that the neck of your ukulele is angled up diagonally, so that you will have comfortable access to your fretboard. Imagine that the elbow of your fretting arm is heavy, ensuring a relaxed arm and elbow.

(a) Good Sitting Posture: Front

(b) Good Sitting Posture: Side

(c) Bad Sitting Posture

FIG. I.4. Sitting

PART I

Chords and How They're Built

Knowing the notes on your fretboard is an essential part of learning the ukulele. In my thirty years of teaching, I have found that far too many students gloss over this vital part of their education. Do not skip this step. Without this, it can be difficult to learn various chord voicings and scales on your instrument. While many students find the prospect of memorizing their fretboard intimidating, it doesn't have to be. The first example shows the notes on each string, up to the 12th fret. If you're not already familiar with the notes on your neck, study this diagram, saying the names of the notes up each fret as you play them.

CHAPTER 1

Notes on the Neck

MAPPING OUT THE NOTES

FIG. 1.1. Notes on Each String

There are a few different things you can do to learn the notes on your neck, beyond just reciting the notes up each fret. One idea is to find a note—any note— once on all strings. Try finding an A note on each string, as shown in figure 1.2.

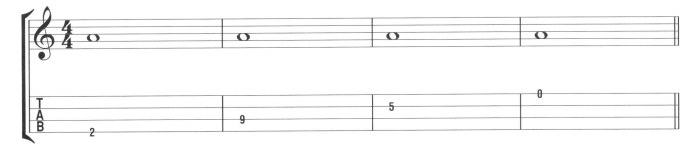

FIG. 1.2. A on Each String

Because of the range of the ukulele, there are some pitches that don't occur in four places. In that case, you can find the octave of that note on another string. The following example shows some of the places that you can play a C note.

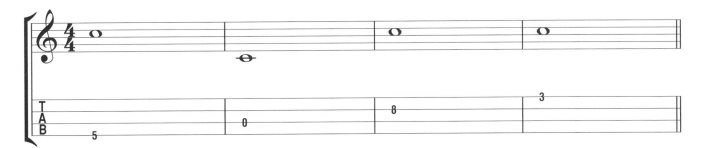

FIG. 1.3. C on Each String

It can be helpful to memorize the notes going across one fret. Figure 1.4 contains the notes going across the 7th fret: D, G, B, and E. When you memorize the notes going across one fret, it can act as a roadmap to the surrounding areas of the fretboard. If you know that D is the 7th fret on the G string, then you can see that C is a whole step down on your 5th fret. E is a whole step higher on the 9th fret.

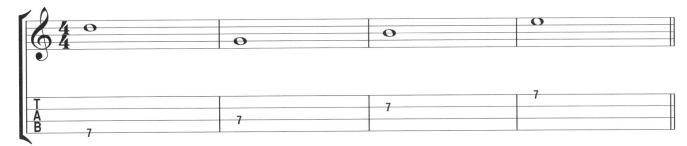

FIG. 1.4. Notes Across the 7th Fret

It can also be helpful to memorize octave and unison shapes on your fretboard in your quest towards memorizing the ukulele neck. In figure 1.5, you'll see two different unison shapes and octave shapes. In the first measure, you'll see that the B on the 2nd fret of the A string is the same pitch as the B on the 4th fret of the G string. If you move that shape up in pitch a half step to your 3rd and 5th frets, you'll have two C notes. If you move it up another fret, you'll have two C♯ or D♭ notes.

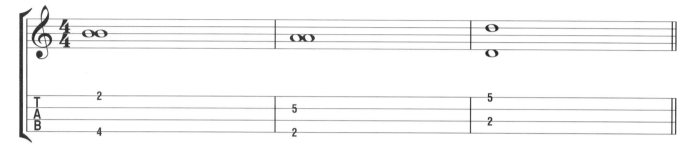

FIG. 1.5. Octave and Unison Shapes

MAPPING MELODIES

Once you have a basic familiarity with the notes on your fretboard, it is a good idea to find out where groups of notes are located in relation to each other. There are several reasons why this is a useful practice.

- It allows you to grab certain notes in easier-to-reach places, as opposed to making big jumps on the fretboard to get to them. This will improve the fluidity in your phrasing.

- When you are playing chord-melody arrangements, there are times where it will be more efficient to grab a particular note in a place that you may not normally play it in. You may be playing a chord voicing on a particular part of the neck, necessitating playing a note in that area.

- Mapping out melodies in different places makes it easier to employ the Campanella technique, as discussed in chapter 4.

One way of doing this is to map out a familiar melody on the ukulele fretboard and then find it in a couple of different places on the ukulele neck.

In figure 1.6, you'll first find "Twinkle, Twinkle Little Star" played on the E and A strings (Version 1). In Version 2, the same melody is played starting in the fifth position. Position playing refers to the fretting hand staying in one place, with each finger assigned to a specific fret. If one is playing in the fifth position, the index finger plays the 5th fret, the middle finger plays the 6th fret, the ring finger plays the 7th fret, and the pinky plays the 8th fret.

FIG. 1.6. Two Versions of "Twinkle, Twinkle Little Star"

For a little more practice with mapping melodies, here are two versions of "Are You Sleeping?" aka "Frère Jacques." The first example stays mostly within the first few frets, with the exception of the D note on the 5th fret of the A string. The second examples stay mostly in the fifth position, with the exception of the open C string.

Version 1

Version 2

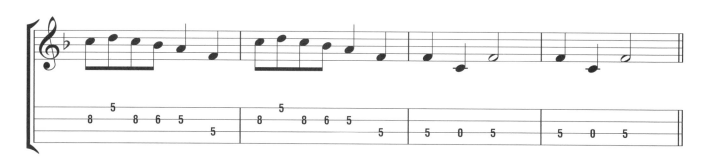

FIG. 1.7. Two Versions of "Are You Sleeping?"

It is important to remember that you will not learn your fretboard overnight. Be patient with yourself, and be consistent with your practice. Even if you dedicate just five minutes of each practice session to building your fretboard knowledge, you will reap the benefits. Transposing to different keys, finding new chord voicings, and learning melodies will be much easier, because you'll know where the notes are located. Learning your fretboard is the first step towards this.

CHAPTER 2

Triads

The first chords most ukulele players learn to play are the basic chords that use open strings combined with fretted notes at the base of the fretboard. C, F, A minor, G, etc. As you progress and want to find new sounds, you will become curious about what chords lie in other parts of the neck. A good way to start exploring your ukulele's fretboard is by learning three-note chords, or *triads*, in other places on the neck. Also, this knowledge of triads will be essential in your development as a solo ukulele player and arranger.

TYPES OF TRIADS

Most of the open chords you probably know are triads, and many popular songs consist solely of these chords, so finding different voicings of them is invaluable. There are four basic kinds of triads: major, minor, diminished, and augmented. To find the notes in any triad, look at the intervals (the distance between two notes) for that chord.

A C major triad is made up of the notes C, E, and G.

- The interval between C and E is a major third (two whole steps).

- The interval between E and G is a minor third (one and a half steps).

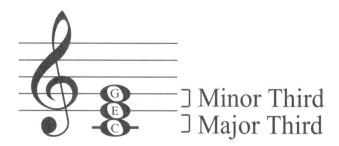

FIG. 2.1. C Major Triad

This relationship between the notes is the same for every major triad.

The C minor triad is made up of the notes C, E♭, and G.

- The interval between C and E♭ is a minor third.

- The interval between E♭ and G is a major third.

Like the other triads, minor triads are all constructed in the same way, with a minor third on the bottom and a major third on top.

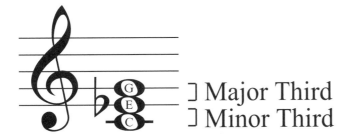

FIG. 2.2. C Minor Triad

Diminished triads are made up of two minor thirds. The notes in a C diminished triad are C, E♭, and G♭.

- The interval between C and E♭ is a minor third.

- The interval between E♭ and G♭ is also a minor third.

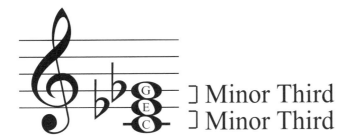

FIG. 2.3. C Diminished Triad

Augmented triads are made up of two major thirds. The notes in a C augmented triad are C, E, and G♯

- The interval between C and E is a major third.

- The interval between E and G♯ is also a major third.

By knowing the intervals that make up the different kinds of triads, you can find the notes of any of these chords on your fretboard.

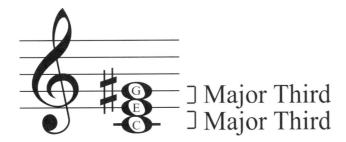

FIG. 2.4. C Augmented Triad

TRIADS, SCALES, AND INTERVALS

An *interval* can be defined as the space, or distance, between two notes. The chords we are discussing in this book are built with either major thirds (two whole steps) or minor thirds (one and a half steps). Since intervals are the building blocks of chords, it is useful to know where to find them on the ukulele. The following exercise shows where you can find major and minor third interval shapes on the E and A strings, C and E strings, and G and A strings.

FIG. 2.5. Major and Minor Thirds on Different String Groupings

Now, let's look at the triads in the C major scale. These are all triads built on each step of the C major scale using only notes in the scale. Studying the major scale triads is helpful because it tells you which chords are likely to be used together in a song, especially if a song you are learning stays in one key. Here are the notes in chords of the C major scale:

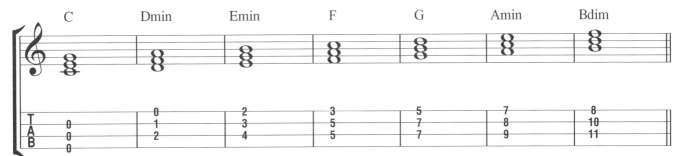

FIG. 2.6. Diatonic Triads in the Key of C

This order of triads is the same for any major scale: the first, fourth, and fifth chords are always major; the second, third, and sixth chord in the series are always minor; and the seventh chord is always diminished.

VOICINGS

To find different *voicings* for these chords (i.e., ways to play them) on the ukulele, start with the open position chords that you are probably already familiar with. Let's start with C major. You might know the open C major chord voicing, consisting of the open G, C, and E strings, with the 3rd fret on the A string. You'll notice that the C note is played both on the open C string and octave up on the 3rd fret of the A string. Because the ukulele has four strings, one of the notes of each triad will be doubled.

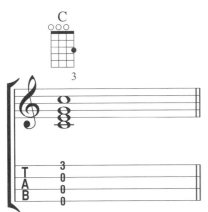

FIG. 2.7. Open C Major Chord

For other possible places to play this chord, look at the chord tones on each string. The open G string is the 5 of C major. The next chord tone you can find on that string would be C, the "1" or the root of the chord. (The chord tones go up in order on each string: root, 3, 5, root, 3, 5, etc.) The C note is on the 5th fret of the G string. That will be the first note in the next voicing of C major. The second note, on the C string, will be your E note, the 3 of the chord, located on your 4th fret. (The previous voicing contained the C, or the root note, on that string.) The next note of the chord, on the E string, will be your G note, or the 5 of the chord, located on the 3rd fret. For the note on the A string, it makes sense to keep the C note on the 3rd fret from the previous chord, to create a chord voicing that's not too much of a stretch for the fingers.

FIG. 2.8. C Major Chord on the 3rd Fret

From here, to find more voicings of C major, simply ascend in order up each string. Since C is the root of the chord, the next higher chord tone on any string will be E (the 3 of the chord). After that comes G (the 5). And up from G will be C again.

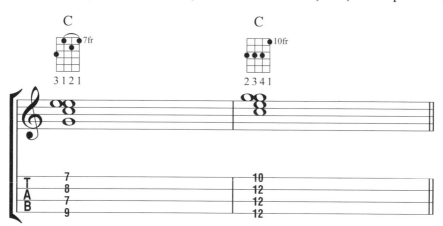

FIG. 2.9. C Major Chords on 7th and 10th Frets

We can use this method to find voicings up the neck of all the other triads as well. See if you can figure out all the voicings up the neck for D minor, E minor, F major, G major, A minor, and B diminished. Learning all these chords will take time, but it is worth the effort. Not only will it help you memorize the fretboard, it will also give you a vast palette of new chord voicings from which to choose from when you want to arrange your favorite tunes. See the chord appendix to check your work!

"AMAZING GRACE"

Let's practice some of these triads by incorporating them into songs. Here is a solo arrangement of "Amazing Grace" using the C major, F major, and G major chords in various positions. With this example, you'll see how important it is to know these voicings up the neck. This knowledge will be invaluable as you begin to develop your own arrangements.

Amazing Grace

Traditional

FIG. 2.10. Amazing Grace

"DOWN IN THE VALLEY"

The traditional song "Down in the Valley" contains the chords F major and C major. You will find a few different voicings of each chord. Strum each chord three times per measure, with the exception of the last F chord. Practice making the transitions between each chord smoothly.

Down in the Valley

Traditional

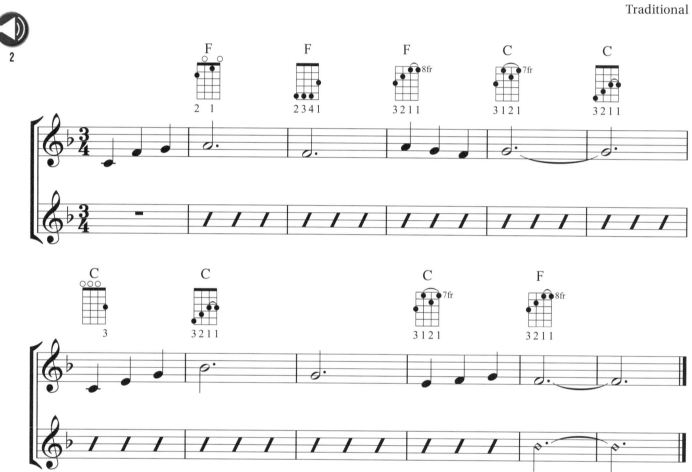

FIG. 2.11. Down in the Valley

"WILL THE CIRCLE BE UNBROKEN"

The classic song "Will the Circle Be Unbroken" contains the G major, C major, D major chords, and E minor chords. As with the previous tune, just strum down strokes. In this case, each chord will get four beats per measure. This will give you practice getting used to switching to these various chords, especially if you are not used to venturing beyond the first few frets. Once this becomes comfortable, you can incorporate different strumming patterns.

Will the Circle Be Unbroken

A.P. Carter,
Charles Hutchinson Gabriel,
and Ada R. Habershon

FIG. 2.12. Will the Circle Be Unbroken

CHAPTER 3

Seventh Chords

You may have noticed that some tunes you have learned contain chords with the number 7 in the name: D7, Gmin7, Cmaj7, etc. While triads are three-note chords, seventh chords are four-note chords. The 7 in the name refers to the seventh degree of the scale, which you are adding, as either the diatonic 7 or a flatted 7 ($\flat$7). Seventh chords offer more color and harmonic variety to your chord progressions.

TYPES OF SEVENTH CHORDS

There are several different types of seventh chords. In this chapter, we will discuss: major 7 chords, dominant 7 chords, minor 7 chords, minor 7$\flat$5 chords (or *half-diminished* 7 chords), and diminished 7 chords.

Let's take a look at *major 7* chords first. In the chapter on triads, we discussed how a major triad is made up of the intervals of a major third and a minor third. To get a major seventh chord, add another major third to the triad. Another way to think about it is to take the first, third, fifth, and seventh notes of the major scale:

C   D   E   F   G   A   B   C
1   2   3   4   5   6   7   8

A C major 7 chord (Cmaj7) is spelled: C, E, G, B.

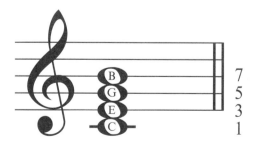

FIG. 3.1. Cmaj7

It is beneficial to look at music theory/concepts in more than one way. Looking at things from the harmony standpoint (intervals) will give you a different understanding than if you just looked at building the chord from the single-notes-from-the-scale perspective. Understanding the relationships between the notes, how they interact with each other, and how this plays out in the music you create is an extremely important part of your development as a musician. Also, if you choose to share your knowledge and the joy of ukulele with others (which I highly encourage you to do!), it is vital to realize that people have different learning styles and ways of processing information. Having the ability to explain the same thing in more than one way can be helpful to any potential students.

A *dominant 7* chord is created when you take a major triad and add a *minor third* to it. The scale degrees (notes from the scale) that form the chord are: 1, 3, 5, ♭7.

C	D	E	F	G	A	B♭	C
1	2	3	4	5	6	♭7	8

A C dominant 7 chord (C7) is spelled: C, E, G, B♭

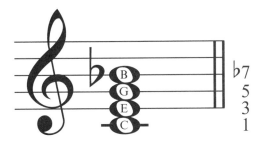

FIG. 3.2. C7

A *minor 7* chord is created when you take a minor triad and add a minor third to it. The scale degrees that form a minor 7 chord are: 1, ♭3, 5, ♭7.

C	D	E♭	F	G	A	B♭	C
1	2	♭3	4	5	6	♭7	8

A C minor 7 (Cmin7) chord is spelled: C, E♭, G, B♭.

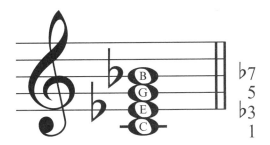

FIG. 3.3. Cmin7

A *minor 7 ♭5* chord (also known as a *half-diminished* seventh chord) is created when you take a diminished triad and add a major third to it. The scale degrees that form a minor 7 ♭5 chord are: 1, ♭3, ♭5, ♭7.

C	D	E♭	F	G♭	A	B♭	C
1	2	♭3	4	♭5	6	♭7	8

A C minor 7 ♭5 chord (Cmin7♭5) is spelled: C, E♭, G♭, and B♭.

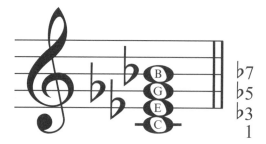

FIG. 3.4. Cmin7♭5

A *diminished 7 chord* occurs when you add a minor third to a diminished triad. The scale degrees that form a diminished 7 chord are: 1, ♭3, ♭5, ♭♭7.

C	D	E♭	F	G♭	A	B♭♭	C
1	2	♭3	4	♭5	6	♭♭7	8

A C diminished 7 chord (Cdim7) is spelled: C, E♭, G♭, and B♭♭ (also known as A).

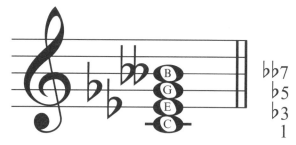

FIG. 3.5. Cdim7

Once you have a basic understanding of how to construct these seventh chords, I urge you to practice finding different voicings of these chords up the neck, just as you did with the triads. Check out the appendix of seventh chords in the back of the book. This knowledge will be indispensable for you as an arranger, accompanist, and your overall mastery of the instrument.

"ST. JAMES INFIRMARY"

"St. James Infirmary" gives you an opportunity to practice some seventh chords. While the melody has been included, the focus here is on learning new chords voicings. However, I strongly encourage you to learn the melody of any song that you are learning, not just the chords. The knowledge of both the melody and the harmony will give you a more complete picture of the song. Some things to consider:

- If there is only one chord in a measure, play each chord four times (quarter notes). Use downstrokes.

- For the measures where there are two chords, play each chord for two beats each. For example, in the first full measure, play Dmin7 for two counts and Gmin7 for two counts.

• If there is no chord above a measure, stick with the chord from the previous measure. For instance, in the third measure, play two counts of Dmin7 and two counts of Gmin7.

St. James Infirmary

Irving Mills

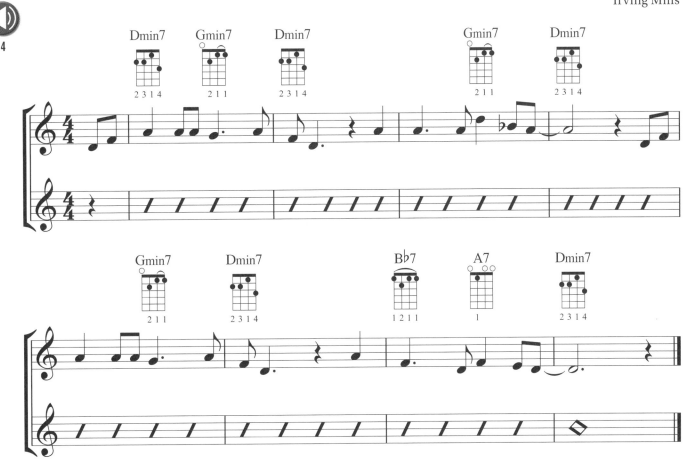

FIG. 3.6. St. James Infirmary

"AVALON"

The next song, "Avalon," employs a wider variety of chords, but the same method of practice still applies. Play the chords as quarter notes or four downstrokes per measure. If there are two chords per measure, play each chord twice. Once again, the melody is included. Notice the relationship between the chords and the melody. For instance, the first note of the first full measure is G, which is the root of the Gmin7. When you get to the C7 chord in measure three, the first melody note is B♭, which is the ♭7 of the chord. Developing this awareness will make finding voicings that fit with the melody easier as you start to create your own arrangements.

Avalon

FIG. 3.7. Avalon

VOICE LEADING

As you expand your chord vocabulary, you may find yourself jumping from one part of the neck to another in a way that does not feel and sound connected. *Voice leading* can create continuity and fluidity in your chord progressions.

You can think about voice leading this way: In addition to thinking about the chord as an independent entity, also think about the separate notes of the chords (the *voices*) and how they lead smoothly to the corresponding note of the next chord.

Let's look at this more closely. Figure 3.9 shows a typical chord progression, but without great voice leading. It should be noted that, because of the range of the ukulele, you have to work pretty hard to not have decent voice leading. However, it is still helpful to be aware of it when creating arrangements.

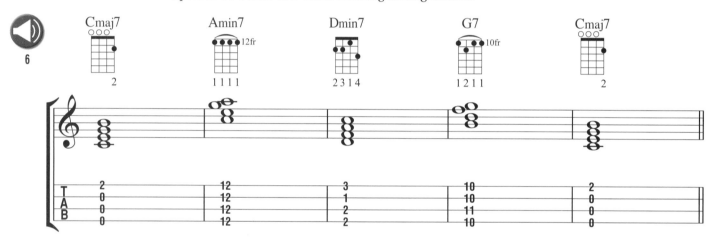

FIG. 3.8. Chord Progression without Good Voice Leading

Figure 3.10 shows the same chord progression, but with some different voicings, providing better voice leading. Notice the stepwise movement between each voice/note of the chord into the next chord. Each note does one of three things: stays the same, moves a whole step, or a half step into a note/voice from the next chord.

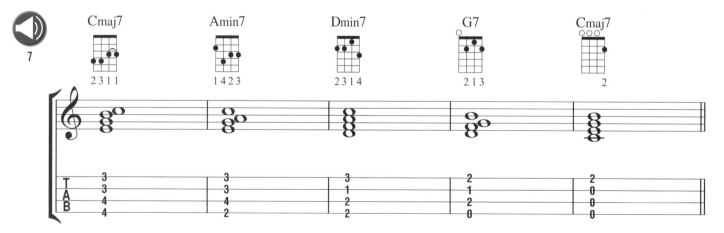

FIG. 3.9. Chord Progression with Good Voice Leading

The next two examples (figures 3.11 and 3.12) show the same chord progression in different places on the neck. Notice both the similarities and the differences of each example. Study the notation and see how each chord moves to the following chord.

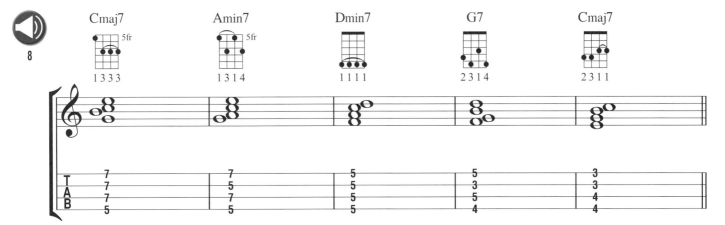

FIG. 3.10. Variation 1 on Chord Progression

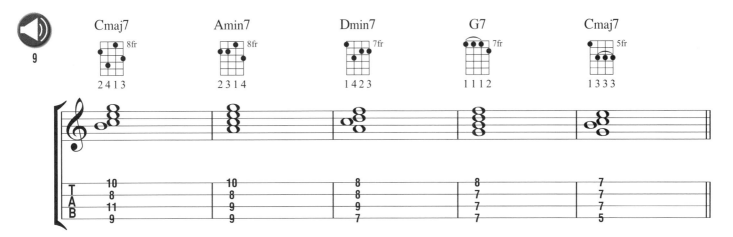

FIG. 3.11. Variation 2 on Chord Progression

"LIMEHOUSE BLUES"

The following chord melody arrangement of "Limehouse Blues" has various voicings of seventh chords all over the neck. Once you get comfortable with the basic arrangement, you can add your own variations to it. Try to keep the chords ringing out and don't lift up from a chord unless you have to. Take, for instance, measure 15, with the D7 chord. Hold the chord down as you reach for the 8th fret of the C string with your pinky. Then, continue to hold the chord down as your third finger plays the 7th fret of the C string. After that, all you have to do is lift up your third finger to get back the original chord position.

Limehouse Blues

Douglas Furber and Philip Braham

FIG. 3.12. Limehouse Blues

PART II

Techniques

The ukulele is a unique, beautiful instrument. Its tonal characteristics offer an opportunity to explore various colors that other stringed instruments don't necessarily provide. The standard tuning for the ukulele utilizes a *reentrant tuning*, where the pitches are not in order from lowest to highest. The banjo is another example of an instrument with reentrant tuning.

CHAPTER 4

Campanella Technique

CAMPANELLA TECHNIQUE

The fourth string, the high G note, allows for a cascading effect to melody playing. When playing a melody in this way, the ukuleleist tries to play the notes in a tune on different strings, letting them ring out together. For instance, if a melody goes from B to C, you might play the B note on the 4th fret of the G string and the C note on the 3rd fret of the A string. This is known as the Campanella technique.

To explore this technique, let's look at some examples of scales played using the Campanella technique. The first example shows a G major scale. Pay attention to the suggested fingerings in this example, and let the notes ring out for as long as possible. The sound of the notes ringing out against each other, and the dissonance they create, is a major component of the Campanella technique. As you practice this example and start to increase the tempo, try to keep the notes ringing out against each other, cascading one into the next. Enjoy the dissonance!

FIG. 4.1. G Major Scale

The next example shows the same technique using an E minor scale. Be conscious of the same things that you practiced in the previous example. Let the notes ring out against each other. Try it with other scales as well!

FIG. 4.2. E Minor Scale

To master this technique, take a melody that you are familiar with. Just as you did in the first chapter with melody mapping, see how many different places you can play the tune on the ukulele fretboard. Purposely try to find notes that are on different strings. Practice playing one phrase of the tune at a time, holding the notes out for as long as possible. Let them ring out against each other.

"ALOHA 'OE"

Let's explore this technique with a song. This arrangement of "Aloha 'Oe" showcases
a melody played with the Campanella technique.

Aloha 'Oe

Lili'uokalani

FIG. 4.3. Aloha 'Oe

"LONDONDERRY AIR"

To incorporate the Campanella technique into your arrangements, one idea is to start with the melody and arrange it, Campanella-style. Then, add a chord any time there is a melody note that is held out for a quarter note or longer. In the following examples, you'll find the tune "Londonderry Air" (aka "Danny Boy"), first arranged solely with the melody, played in the Campanella style. The example after that is another rendition of the same song, this time with chords added. This can also be used to build longer arrangements. For instance, try playing "Londonderry Air" with just the melody and then lead directly into the version with the chords.

Londonderry Air
Melody Only

Traditional

FIG. 4.4. "Londonderry Air" Melody Played with the Campanella Technique

Melody with Chords

FIG. 4.5. "Londonderry Air" with Chords

CHAPTER 5

Fingerstyle Patterns

The ukulele is a wonderful instrument for exploring fingerstyle technique. In fingerstyle ukulele, you pluck notes of a chord individually as opposed to strumming them simultaneously. In instrumental fingerstyle arrangements, the melody is incorporated into the fingerstyle pattern. The result of the chordal accompaniment with the melody being combined into the fingerstyle pattern allows for the possibility of beautiful solo arrangements on the uke. You can be a one-person band!

Efficiency of movement in your picking hand is important. Assign a finger to each string. This will help to minimize unnecessary movement and promote fluidity in your fingerstyle technique. To notate which fingers to use on your picking hand, we will employ the nomenclature used in classical guitar. The letters used stand for the Spanish words for these fingers: *pulgar, indice, medio,* and *anular: p, i, m,* and *a.* The pinky is generally not used.

Finger	Spanish Name	Symbol
thumb	pulgar	*p*
index finger	indice	*i*
middle finger	medio	*m*
ring finger	anular	*a*

Proper position of the picking hand is important for optimal tone and to avoid injury. Loosely curl your fingers in, but leave the thumb sticking out. Bring the fingers to the string, with the thumb closer to the fretboard than the other fingers.

FIG. 5.1. Fingerstyle Position

PATTERNS IN 4/4 TIME

The first example uses the thumb on the G and C string, the index on the E string, and the middle finger on the A string.

FIG. 5.2. Fingerstyle Pattern 1: *ppim*

This next example uses the same picking-hand fingering, but with a more varied pattern.

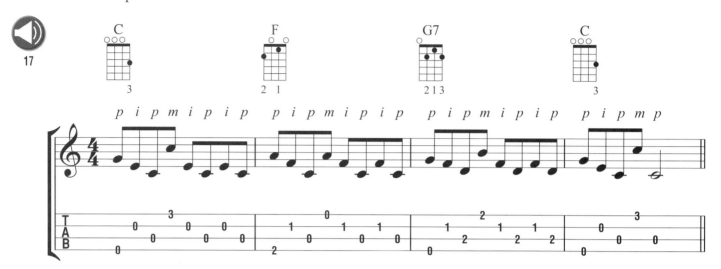

FIG. 5.3. Fingerstyle Pattern 2: *pipmipip*

The third example incorporates plucking two strings at once, and we've added the ring finger to play the A string. Try to get an even tone between all of the strings.

FIG. 5.4. Fingerstyle Pattern 3: *mp i am i*

This next example is similar to a banjo roll. These cascading figures sound great once you work them up to speed.

FIG. 5.5. Fingerstyle Pattern 4: *mip*

"LUNA'S SONG"

The following piece incorporates all of these patterns and utilizes a wider variety of chords.

Luna's Song

Karen Hogg

FIG. 5.6. Luna's Song

PATTERNS IN 3/4 TIME

Next up, we have some patterns in 3/4 time. The first example is simple, arpeggiating through basic chords using the thumb, index, middle, and ring fingers.

FIG. 5.7. Fingerstyle Pattern 1 in 3/4: *pimami*

The next example has you plucking up to three strings at a time. Like previous examples, try to even out your tone. Make sure none of the notes sound louder than the others.

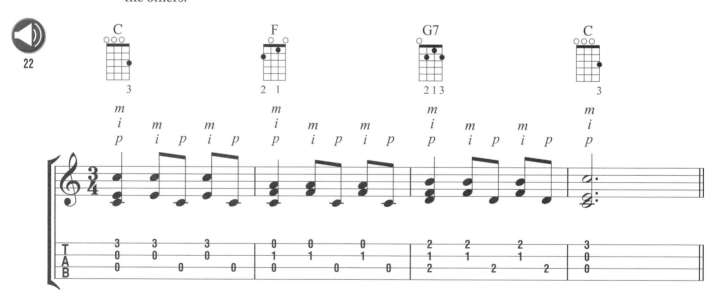

FIG. 5.8. Fingerstyle Pattern 2 in 3/4: *mip mi p mi p*

The last example in 3/4 incorporates a sixteenth-note pattern.

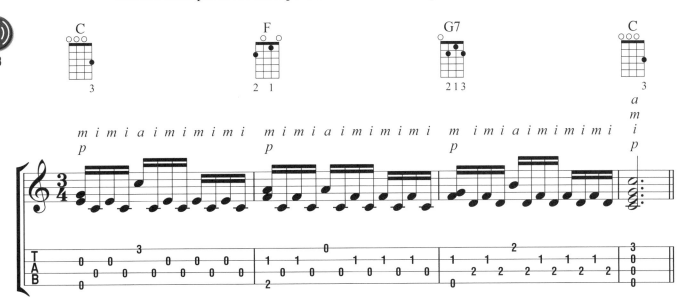

FIG. 5.9. Fingerstyle Pattern 3 in 3/4: *mp i mi a i m i m i m i*

"A MINOR UKULELE WALTZ"

This waltz incorporates all of these patterns in 3/4.

A Minor Ukulele Waltz

Karen Hogg

FIG. 5.10. A Minor Ukulele Waltz

CHAPTER 6

Tremolo

There are several types of techniques that may be known more on other stringed instruments, but they also sound great on the ukulele. Tremolo is no exception. It is commonly associated with the classical guitar. Tremolo is achieved by playing the same note repeatedly with different fingers, creating a sound of continuity between the notes.

The following example shows the typical way that many classical guitarists approach tremolo: *pami*, with the thumb playing the accompaniment on another string, followed the ring, middle, and index fingers playing a repeated melody note on a higher string.

Bring your picking hand to the ukulele. Place your thumb on the G string. The rest of your fingers should be gently curled in toward the palm of your hand. Pluck the G string with a downward motion of the thumb. As soon as the G strings sounds out, place your ring finger (*anular*) on the A string, plucking the string and bringing the ring finger toward the palm of the hand. Then, immediately place your middle finger on the A string, plucking it and bringing the middle finger toward the palm of your hand. Finally, place the index finger on the A string, plucking the string and bringing the index finger toward the palm of your hand. Repeat.

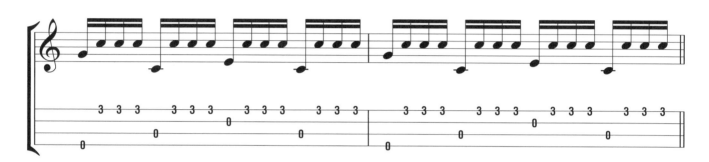

FIG. 6.1. Tremolo with Classical Guitar Approach: *pami*

The next example continues to explore tremolo with the added challenge of various chord changes.

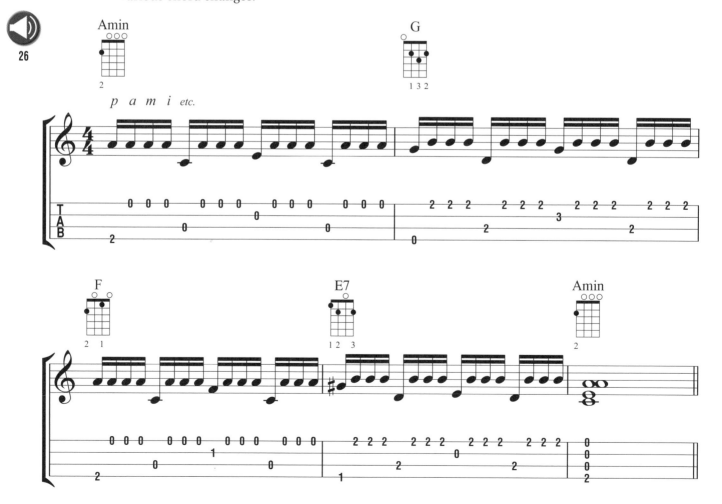

FIG. 6.2. Tremolo on Different Chords Changes

While this is the way tremolo is usually played on a classical guitar, some ukuleleists take a different approach, leaving out the ring finger. For instance, you can play the previous example using *p*, *i*, *m*, *i*, etc. Personally, I like the classical guitar approach. I feel like the sound is more fluid. However, it is always best to experiment with various approaches and find which one works best for your style.

It takes time to develop a smooth, even-sounding tremolo. With patience and consistent practice, it can be done!

- **Keep an even rhythm.** Start slowly. Think about counting the subdivisions out loud to ensure that you are playing evenly: 1e&a, 2e&a, 3e&a, 4e&a, etc.

- **Work with a metronome.** Practicing with a metronome is helpful no matter what technique you are trying to master. With tremolo, playing with a metronome is a great way to incrementally increase speed while ensuring steady rhythm. Pick a tempo/metronome marking where you can play the examples and song from this chapter at a comfortable, relaxed pace. As you gain more confidence, slowly increase the tempo. Resist the urge to play quickly before you are ready to. This will result in less-than-optimal tone and a possible build-up of tension in your hand. It is much better to slowly work up the tempo of tremolo over time. You'll get there!

- **Nails.** Your nails should be the same length on each finger. It's a good idea to regularly file them into a rounded, smooth shape. That way, parts of your nail don't get caught on the string. Also, this helps with evenness of tone.

"ODE TO JOY"

Now, let's apply the tremolo technique to Beethoven's "Ode to Joy." Try it both with *pami* and *pimi*.

Ode to Joy

Ludwig van Beethoven

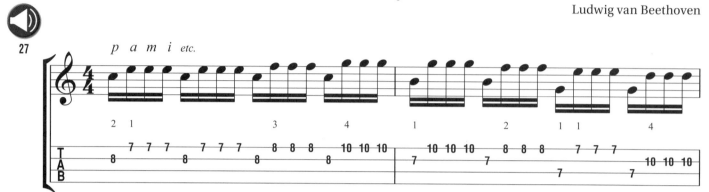

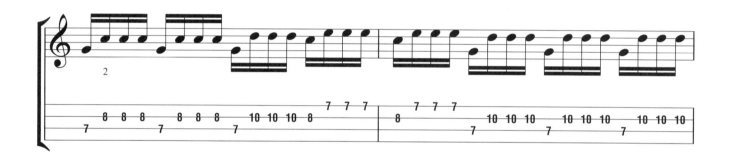

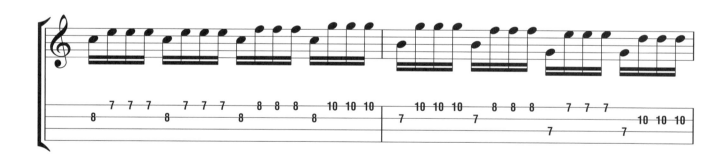

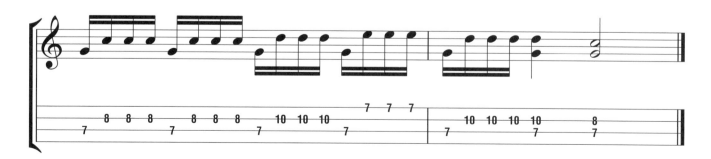

FIG. 6.3. "Ode to Joy" with Tremolo Fingering

CHAPTER 7

Harmonics

Harmonics are the bell-like effect created when a ukuleleist places a finger right above a fret in a particular place on the ukulele and plucks that string. There are two types of harmonics: natural and artificial. *Natural harmonics* occur when you lightly place a finger right over (for example) the 12th fret of the ukulele, without fretting the note, and pluck. Make sure to *barely* touch the string. If you press too hard, the harmonic will not sound out. Depending on the ukulele, you can sometimes get natural harmonics on the 5th and 7th frets as well.

FIG. 7.1. Natural Harmonics

Artificial harmonics occur when you fret a note normally with your fretting hand. Then, you place a finger (usually the index finger of your picking hand) on a fret that is exactly twelve frets above the initial note that you fretted. For instance, if you are fretting the 1st fret of your A string, you want to go the 13th fret of the A string to get the artificial harmonic. Place the pad—not the tip—of your picking-hand index finger directly over the 13th fret. With the thumb of your picking hand, pluck the A string. It takes some patience, but once you get it, it will sound lovely.

FIG. 7.2. Artificial Harmonics

The following example is a C major scale played with artificial harmonics. The regular notes that you need to fret are in the tablature. Above the tab is the fret placement required to get the artificial harmonic.

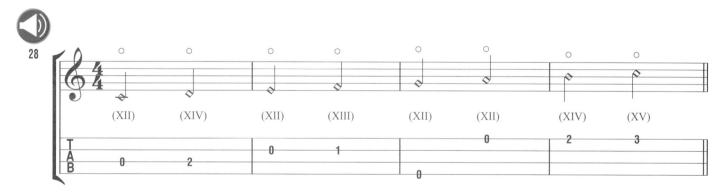

FIG. 7.3. C Major Scale with Harmonics

The following example shows how you can play arpeggios with harmonics. Finger each chord for one measure, playing the harmonic of each note one octave up from it. Ukulele players like John King have used this technique.

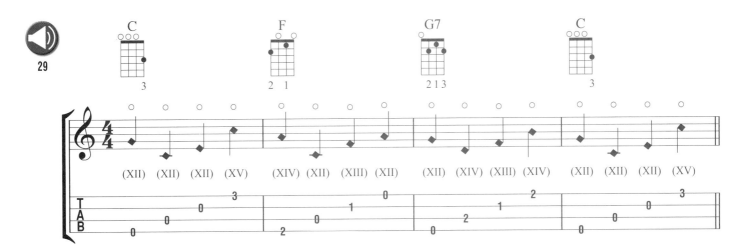

FIG. 7.4. Arpeggios with Harmonics

The following example employs both regular notes and harmonics played together. Here's where things can get a little tricky. The first two notes played together are the open C and open E strings. The E string should be played as a harmonic. Instead of the thumb plucking the harmonic with the picking hand, use your ring finger.

FIG. 7.5. Harmonic and a Note

You will be doing three things with your picking hand:

1. Placing the pad of your index finger over the 12th fret on the E string.

2. Plucking the open C string with your thumb.

3. Plucking the E string 12th fret harmonic with your ring finger.

This will take practice to develop coordination. Have patience! You can do it. This is a technique that the late John King used in his ukulele arrangements, including his beautiful rendition of "Jesu, Joy of Man's Desiring."

30

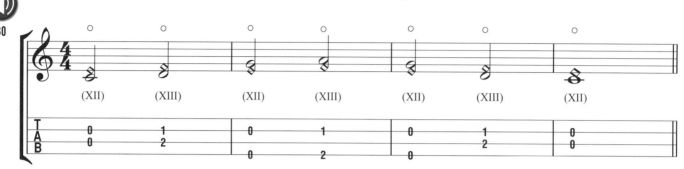

FIG. 7.6. Harmonics and Regular Notes Together

"SHENANDOAH"

Here is an arrangement of the traditional song "Shenandoah," with a few artificial harmonics tastefully placed in the tune. Like the example above, these harmonics are played simultaneously with regular fretted notes.

Shenandoah

Traditional

FIG. 7.7. Shenandoah

CHAPTER 8

Clawhammer

Clawhammer banjo is a picking style that is especially popular in old-time music. It differs from the Scruggs style of playing in the direction of the picking. Clawhammer is a primarily down-picked style. It can be both highly rhythmic and melodic at the same time.

The ukulele, with its high G string, is also a good instrument for clawhammer! To practice clawhammer, curl the fingers of your picking hand, as if you are about to make a gentle fist. Do not close the fist entirely. Stay relaxed.

FIG. 8.1. Clawhammer Hand Position

To play the example in figure 8.2, strike the melody note on the A string with the back part of your curled index finger. Think about hitting the string with the nail bed part of your finger. Then, hit the E and C strings, again with the back part of your index, followed by your thumb plucking the G string. It is not important if you end up hitting more than the E and C string on the second strike. The driving rhythm is more important: 1 2& 3 4&, etc. In measures 2 and 4, pluck the open C string and hammer-on (**H**) to the 2nd fret of that string. Once you pluck the open C string, forcefully bring the second finger for your fretting hand onto the fretboard, right before the 2nd fret.

For players who are used to other picking styles, hitting the strings with the back part of your finger might take getting used to, but it is essential to get the propulsive feel of clawhammer.

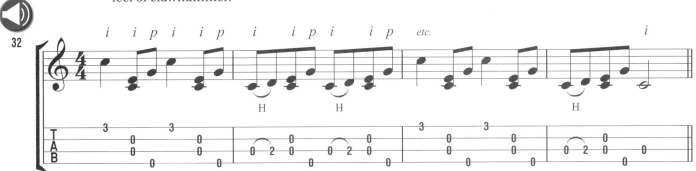

FIG. 8.2. Clawhammer Example 1: *iip*

Figure 8.3 starts off with the same rhythmic elements as the previous example, moving into a bluesy line in the second measure. You can either slide or hammer-on from the D to the E♭ in measure 3 and 4.

FIG. 8.3. Clawhammer Example 2

"BOIL THEM CABBAGE DOWN"

Now, let's take the old fiddle tune "Boil Them Cabbage Down," and play it clawhammer style. Be steady with your rhythm. Don't worry about playing it fast immediately. Play it slowly and then gradually work up the speed.

Boil Them Cabbage Down

Traditional

FIG. 8.4. Boil Them Cabbage Down

"CRAWDAD SONG"

The next piece, "Crawdad Song," incorporates a melody that moves around a little more. Do your best to keep the propulsive rhythm, while also making sure the melody is clear.

Crawdad Song

Traditional

FIG. 8.5. Crawdad Song

CHAPTER 9

Arranging

Now that you have a greater understanding of your fretboard, a bigger chord vocabulary, and some cool techniques under your belt, you can begin to come up with your own arrangements. While it can seem daunting, if you follow a few simple steps, you'll be an expert arranger before you know it!

KNOW THE MELODY

This is your first step. If you don't know the melody, you can't create an arrangement. Either get the sheet music for the song you want to arrange or figure out the melody by ear. Once you have the melody, the next question to ask yourself is what key you should put it in. You want to play it in a key that lays well on the ukulele. The melody has to be in the range of the ukulele. Remember that the lowest note on the ukulele, if it is tuned to standard pitch, is the open C string. So, the lowest note of the melody cannot dip below C. And then, the highest note of the melody cannot extend beyond whatever the top pitch of your ukulele is. Once you have decided what key you are going to put the melody in, write it out.

"HARD TIMES COME AGAIN NO MORE"

Let's explore some ways we can arrange "Hard Times Come Again No More." First, let's look at the melody. It's in the key of G. The lowest note is D, on the 2nd fret of the C string. The highest note is G, which can be played on the 10th fret of the A string. The tune sits nicely on the uke in this key.

Hard Times Come Again No More

Stephen Foster

FIG. 9.1. "Hard Times Come Again No More" Original Melody

HARMONIZE THE MELODY

After you have learned the melody, the real fun of arranging begins. The next step is to harmonize the melody. To do this, first look at some of the intervals you can choose from. An interval is the space, or the distance between two notes. The color of the interval will change depending on how small or large it is. Here are some possible intervals to use when developing your arrangements:

Interval	Steps	Example from G
minor second	a half step	G to A♭
major second	a whole step	G to A
minor third	one and a half steps	G to B♭
major third	two whole steps	G to B
perfect fourth	two and a half steps	G to C
tritone augmented fourth diminished fifth	three whole steps	G to C♯
perfect fifth	three and a half steps	G to D
minor sixth	four whole steps	G to E♭
major sixth	four and a half steps	G to E
minor seventh	five whole steps	G to F
major seventh	five and a half steps	G to F♯
octave	six whole steps	G to G

There are certainly larger intervals possible on the ukulele, but this information is a good starting point. The following example shows some different places that you can play these intervals on the ukulele. The placement of the intervals changes on the second line, to illustrate another way you can play the same intervals.

FIG. 9.2. Intervals in Various Positions

One thing to remember is that it is important to have the melody take center stage. If the listener cannot pick up the melody in the arrangement, then you may want to rethink your arrangement.

Figure 9.3 is an arrangement using just intervals to harmonize the melody of "Hard Times Come Again No More." Remember that your note choices are just that, choices. You can think of harmony like a painter would think about colors. Different colors/sounds evoke different emotions. The sounds you create don't necessarily have to be pretty. The arrangement below is just one way you can play this tune. I encourage you to experiment with a wide variety of note choices and see what you come up with!

Hard Times Come Again No More

Stephen Foster

FIG. 9.3. "Hard Times Come Again No More" Harmonized with Intervals

Next, we can begin to build on the harmony by thinking about different chords we can play. The next version of "Hard Times..." is built mostly around triads, with one dominant seventh chord thrown in. Notice the difference in the sound.

FIG. 9.4. "Hard Times Come Again No More" Harmonized with Triads

Next, let's take it a step further and make the harmony a little more lush. The next arrangement of the tune employs various seventh chords. Again, notice the difference in the sound when using different note choices.

FIG. 9.5. "Hard Times Come Again No More" Harmonized with Seventh Chords

For fun, and to show how you can apply one of the techniques we talked about in your arrangements, here is one more version of "Hard Times Come Again No More," arranged with clawhammer picking. Go back and play through the other arrangements of this tune before you try this one. Notice the differences. Try to arrange a song you like in several different ways, experimenting with different chords, rhythms, and techniques. The creative possibilities are endless!

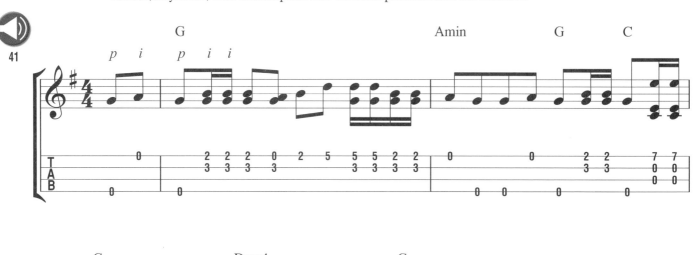

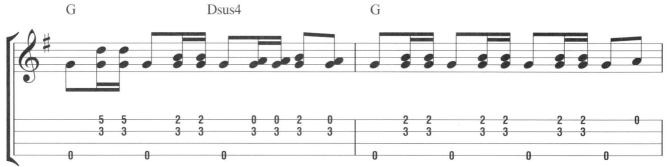

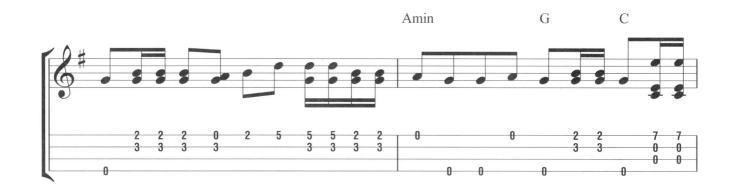

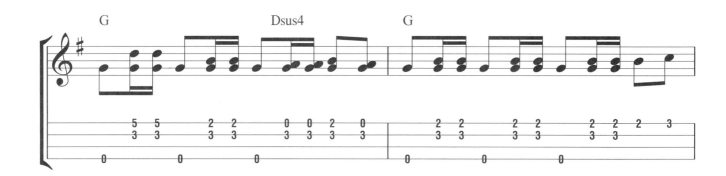

FIG. 9.6. "Hard Times Come Again No More" Clawhammer Style

IN CONCLUSION

Learning the ukulele, like learning any instrument, is a lifetime journey. My hope is that this book gave you some food for thought and plenty of help on the journey to becoming a better ukulele player!

APPENDIX

TRIADS

SEVENTH CHORDS

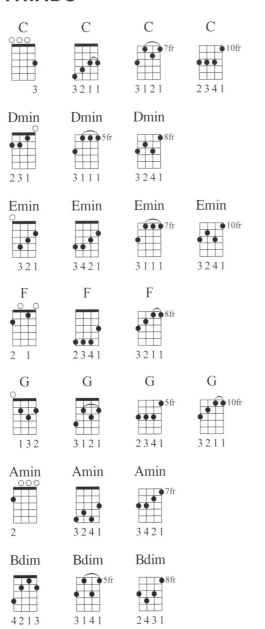

FIG. A.1. Triads

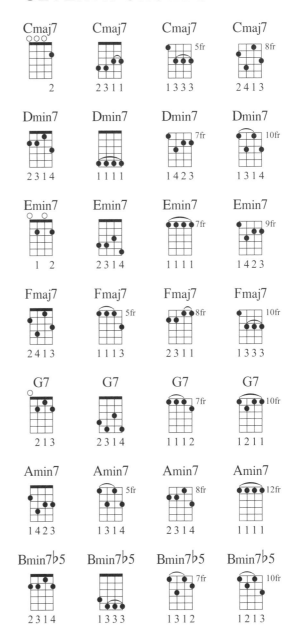

FIG. A.2. Seventh Chords

68

ABOUT THE AUTHOR

Photo by Tracy Walton

Karen Hogg is a multi-instrumentalist, educator, and writer living in southern Connecticut. Hogg has been teaching music since 1990 and has written two instructional books for guitar: *Women in Rock* and *Guitar Made Easy* (Alfred Publishing). Additionally, she is the author of numerous articles and lessons for publications such as *Acoustic Guitar Magazine*, *Fretboard Journal*, and *She Shreds*.